Footprints OF THE FUTURE

Footprints OF THE FUTURE

A Youth Journal

Dr. Wesley Proctor

Printed in the United States of America

Publishing services by Selah Publishing Group, LLC, Tennessee. The views expressed or implied in this work do not necessarily reflect those of Selah Publishing Group.

ISBN: 978-1-58930-236-5
Library of Congress Control Number: 2009903403

I would like to dedicate this book to:

Every young person – **YOU CAN MAKE IT!!!!**

Elder Brian and Deaconess Pamela Williams - Thank you for believing in me and for everything you have done to help me with this project. I will never forget your kindness.

Contents

Foreword

Everyone on their earthly journey needs to commune with God, and this includes Young People. I am glad that God has placed it in the heart of my son, Dr. Wesley Proctor, to pen a book designed to be a source of help and inspiration for those who find it difficult to navigate through the rough edges of life. What I love about the book is that it is easy to understand. It is not so technical that a young person can't understand it.

Young man and young lady, get ready to be blessed as you have in your hands a devotional created just for you!!!

Bishop Jimmie A. Ellis, III
Founder & Pastor
Victory Christian Center of Philadelphia

ANGER

We all know what anger is and how it feels to be angry. Many young people carry anger within their hearts and never learn how to overcome it God's way. God's ultimate plan for us is to show compassion towards each other.

1. **When you become angry, THINK "before" you react.**

   Proverbs 29:1 - The man who is often reproved but refuses to accept criticism will suddenly be broken and never have another chance.

2. **If you answer gently without anger, you will help deflate the situation.**

   Proverbs 15:1 - A gentle answer turns away wrath, but harsh words cause quarrels.

Proverbs 15:18 **-** A quick-tempered man starts fights; a cool-tempered man tries to stop them.

Proverbs 20:22 **-** Don't repay evil for evil. Wait for the Lord to handle the matter.

3. **When you become angry, work quickly to resolve the matter.**

Ephesians 4:26 **-** If you are angry, don't sin by nursing your grudge. Don't let the sun go down with you still angry. Get over it quickly;

4. **Demonstrate patience, which is the opposite of anger.**

Proverbs 14:29 **-** A wise man controls his temper. He knows that anger causes mistakes.

Proverbs 15:18 **-** A quick-tempered man starts fights; a cool-tempered man tries to stop them.

???? Questions To Consider ????

1. When you've been angry, what was the cause??

____

____

____

____

____

2. How did you handle the situation??

____

____

____

____

____

3. What could you have done differently??

____

____

____

____

____

ATTITUDE

1. **Loving God will help us maintain a positive attitude.**

   Deuteronomy 10:12-13 – And now, Israel, what does the Lord your God require of you except to listen carefully to all He says to you, and to obey for your own good the commandments I am giving you today, and to love Him, and to worship Him with all your hearts and souls?

   Matthew 22:37 - Jesus replied, "Love the Lord your God with all your heart, soul, and mind. This is the first and greatest commandment. The second most important is similar: 'Love your neighbors as much as you love yourself'".

2. **Our attitudes should be focused on SPIRITUAL things, considering how we may please God.**

   Romans 8:5-8 - Those who let themselves be controlled by their lower natures live only to please themselves, but those who follow after the Holy Spirit find themselves doing those things that please God. Following after the Holy Spirit leads to life and peace, but following after the old nature leads to death, because the old sinful nature within us is against God. It never did obey God's laws and it never will. That's why those who are still under the control of their old sinful selves, bent on following their old evil desires, can never please God.

3. **Our minds must be renewed and transformed by the power of God. We cannot think the same way as unbelievers.**

   Romans 12:2 - Don't copy the behavior and customs of this world, but be a new and different person with a fresh newness in all you do and think. Then you will learn from your own experience how His ways will really satisfy you.

   Ephesians 4:17-18 - Let me say this, then, speaking for the Lord: Live no longer as the unsaved do, for they are blinded and confused. Their closed hearts are full of darkness; they are far away from the life of God because they have shut their minds against Him, and they cannot understand His ways.

Ephesians 4:22-24 - then throw off your old evil nature-the old you that was a partner in your evil ways – rotten through and through, full of lust and sham. Now your attitudes and thoughts must all be constantly changing for the better. Yes, you must be a new and different person, holy and good. Clothe yourself with this new nature.

4. **We should always be considerate of others and place them ahead of ourselves.**

John 15:13 - Greater love hath no man than this that a man lay down his life for his friends.

Philippians 2:3, 5-7 - Don't be selfish; don't live to make a good impression on others. Be humble, thinking of others as better than yourself. Your attitude should be the kind that was shown us by Jesus Christ, who, though He was God, did not demand and cling to His rights as God, but laid aside His might, power and glory, taking the disguise of a slave and becoming like men.

5. **Prayer will help keep our thoughts in proper perspective.**

Philippians 4:6-8 **-** Don't worry about anything; instead, pray about everything; tell God your needs and don't forget to thank Him for His answers. If you do this you will experience God's peace, which is far more wonderful than the human mind can understand. His peace will keep your thoughts and your hearts quiet and at rest as you trust in Christ Jesus. And now, brothers, as I close this letter let me say this one more thing: Fix your thoughts on what is true and good and right. Think about things that are pure and lovely, and dwell on the fine, good things in others. Think about all you can praise God for and be glad about.

???? Questions To Consider ????

Do you think you have a positive attitude about life??

____

____

____

____

____

In what ways can you improve your attitude??

____

____

____

____

____

BITTERNESS

Bitterness is one of the most crushing mental problems in a person's life. When a Christian is bitter, there is a loss of close fellowship with the Lord. Bitterness becomes a hindrance in our relationship with Christ.

1. **Bitterness has a negative impact on us AND those around us.**

   Hebrews 12:15 - Look after each other so that not one of you will fail to find God's best blessings. Watch out that nobitterness takes root among you, for as it springs up it causes deep trouble, hurting many in their spiritual lives.

2. **Bitterness can be eliminated through compassion and forgiveness.**

Ephesians 4:31-32 - Stop being mean, bad-tempered and angry. Quarreling, harsh words, and dislike of others should have no place in your lives. Instead, be kind to each other, tenderhearted, forgiving one another, just as God has forgiven you because you belong to Christ.

???? Questions To Consider ????

Is there bitterness in your heart?? If so, what is the cause??

How does the Bible instruct us to handle bitterness??

Have you ever been around someone who was bitter?? How did it make you feel???

CHOICES &
MAKING DECISIONS

1. **Prayer should be the foundation for every decision we make.**

   Psalm 25:4-5 - Show me the path where I should go, O Lord; point out the right road for me to walk. Lead me; teach me; for you are the God who gives me salvation. I have no hope except in you.

   Jeremiah 10:23 - O Lord, I know it is not within the power of man to map his life and plan his course.

   James 1:5 - If you want to know what God wants you to do, ask Him, and He will gladly tell you, for He is always ready to give a bountiful supply of wisdom to all who ask Him; He will not resent it.

2. **Knowing God's will requires a submissive heart.**

   Psalm 40:8 - And I delight to do your will, my God, for your law is written upon my heart!!

3. **When our hearts are yielded to God, He gives us direction.**

   Proverbs 4:11-13 - I would have you learn this great fact: that a life of doing right is the wisest life there is. If you live that kind of life, you'll not limp or stumble as you run. Carry out my instructions; don't forget them, for they will lead you to real living.

   Psalm 48:14 - For this great God is our God forever and ever. He will be our guide until we die.

   Proverbs 3:4-6 - If you want favor with both God and man, and a reputation for good judgment and common sense, then trust the Lord completely; don't ever trust yourself. In everything you do, put God first, and he will direct you and crown your efforts with success.

4. **Never make decisions that are contrary to God's Word.**

Deuteronomy 5:29 - Oh, that they would always have such a heart for me, wanting to obey my commandments. Then all would go well with them in the future, and with their children throughout all generations!!!

Isaiah 55:8 - This plan of mine is not what you would work out, neither are my thought the same as yours!!!

2 Timothy 3:16-17 - The whole Bible was given to us by inspiration from God and is useful to teach us what is true and to make us realize what is wrong in our lives; it straightens us out and helps us do what is right. It is God's way of making us well prepared at every point, fully equipped to do good to everyone.

???? Questions To Consider ????

Have you made decisions without wise counsel??

What could be some results of making decisions without God??

Can you think of someone from the Bible who acted without consulting God?? What were the consequences??

FORGIVING OTHERS

When we forgive those who hurt us, we are doing more than simply telling them we aren't angry anymore. We are saying we are ready to move beyond the situation and heal. Forgiveness does not erase the wrong that was done. It is a way of recognizing that we **ALL** make mistakes. When we forgive, we are refusing to allow the mistake to ruin the relationship.

1. **God has forgiven us, so we must forgive others. He is our example.**

   Psalm 130:3-4 - Lord, if you keep in mind our sins then who can ever get an answer to his prayers? But you forgive!! What an awesome thing this is!!

   Romans 8:1-2 - So there is now no condemnation awaiting those who belong to Christ Jesus. For the power of the life- giving Spirit – and this power is mine through Christ Jesus – has freed me from the vicious circle of sin and death.

2. **Forgiveness is NOT an option. We MUST forgive. It is written in the Word of God.**

Matthew 5:23-24 **-** So if you are standing before the altar inthe Temple, offering a sacrifice to God, and suddenly remember that a friend has something against you, leave your sacrifice there beside the altar and go and apologize and be reconciled to him, and then come and offer your sacrifice to God.

Matthew 6:9-15 **-** Pray along these lines: "Our Father in heaven, we honor your holy name. We ask that your kingdom will come now, may your will be done here on earth, just as it is in heaven. Give us our food again today, as usual, and forgive us our sins, just as we have forgiven those who have sinned against us. Don't bring us into temptation, but deliver us from the evil one. Amen. Your heavenly Father will forgive you if you forgive those who sin against you; but if you refuse to forgive them, He will not forgive you.

Ephesians 4:32 **-** Instead, be kind to each other, tenderhearted, forgiving one another, just as God has forgiven you because you belong to Christ.

3. **There is no limit to the times we are to forgive.**

Matthew 18:21-22 **-** Then Peter came to him and asked, “Sir, how often should I forgive a brother who sins against me? Seven times? “No!!” Jesus replied, “seventy times seven!!

Luke 17:3-4 **-** “Rebuke your brother if he sins, and forgive him if he is sorry. Even if he wrongs you seven times a day and each time turns again and asks forgiveness, forgive him.”

???? Questions To Consider ????

Do you have difficulty forgiving others who hurt you??

If the person who harmed you acknowledged their wrong and apologized, would that make it easier for you to forgive them??

When it comes to forgiveness, do you operate under the "three strikes and you're out" philosophy??

Have **YOU** harmed someone and now want to be forgiven??

____
____
____
____
____

How would you feel if God or the person you've injured refused to forgive you??

____
____
____
____
____

OBEDIENCE

1. **God requires all young people to be in submission to their parents.**

   Proverbs 6:20 - Young man, obey your father and your mother.

   Ephesians 6:2-3 - Honor your father and mother. This is the first of God's Ten Commandments that ends with a promise. And this is the promise: that if you honor your father and mother, yours will be a long life, full of blessing.

   Colossians 3:20 - You children must always obey your fathers and mothers, for that pleases the Lord.

2. **God has established authority to maintain order in the earth.**

   Romans 13:1, 4-5 - Obey the government, for God is the one who has put it there. There is no government anywhere that God has not placed in power. The policeman is sent by God to help you. But if you are doing something wrong, of course you should be afraid, for he will have you punished. He is sent by God for that very purpose. Obey the laws, then, for two reasons: first, to keep from being punished, and second, just because you know you should.

3. **We must submit to church leadership.**

   Hebrews 13:17 - Obey your spiritual leaders and be willing to do what they say. For their work is to watch over your souls, and God will judge them on how well they do this. Give them reason to report joyfully about you to the Lord and not with sorrow, for then you will suffer for it too.

   1 Thessalonians 5:12-13 - Dear brothers, honor the officers of your church who work hard among you and warn you against all that is wrong. Think highly of them and give them your wholehearted love because they are straining to help you. And remember, no quarreling among yourselves.

4. **All Christians must submit to God. He is the ultimate authority.**

Jeremiah 7:23 **-** But what I told them was: obey me and I will be your God and you shall be my people; only do as I say and all shall be well!!

John 15:10-11 **-** When you obey me you are living in my love, just as I obey my Father and live in His love. I have told you this so that you will be filled with my joy. Yes, your cup of joy will overflow!

1 Peter 1:14-15 **-** Obey God because you are His children; don't slip back into your old ways – doing evil because you knew no better. But be holy now in everything you do, just as the Lord is holy, who invited you to be His child.

???? Questions To Consider ????

Do you have trouble submitting to authority?? If so, why???

____

____

____

____

____

Why did God institute authority??

____

____

____

____

____

Is it okay to rebel against an authority figure because you don't like them??

____

____

____

____

____

How should you handle it if a person abuses/misuses the authority that has been invested in them??

____

____

____

____

____

PRAYER

We all long to connect with someone who can identify with our circumstances and understand our feelings. Our heavenly Father knows and understands us and prayer is what connects us to Him.

1. **Prayer is the foundation of our relationship with God. We MUST do it!!!!**

   Luke 18:1 - One day Jesus told His disciples a story to illustrate their need for constant prayer and to show themthat they must keep praying until the answer comes.

   1 Thessalonians 5:17 - Always keep on praying.

2. **We can pray to God about anything!!**

   Philippians 4:6-7 - Don't worry about anything; instead, pray about everything; tell God your needs and don't forget to thank Him for His answers. If you do this you will experience God's peace, which is far more wonderful than the humanmind can understand. His peace will keep your thoughts and your hearts quiet and at rest as you trust in Christ Jesus.

3. **We are to pray for others.**

John 17 – Read the entire chapter.

Philippians 1:9 - My prayer for you is that you will overflow more and more with love for others, and at the same time keep on growing in spiritual knowledge and insight,

???? QUESTIONS TO CONSIDER ????

Do you pray on a regular/consistent basis??

____

____

____

____

____

Are there issues in your life that you are afraid to discuss with God??

____

____

____

____

____

Do you believe that God knows EVERYTHING about you and longs to help you deal with any problems you are facing??

____

____

____

____

____

Do you pray for others??

____

____

____

____

____

About the Author

Dr. Wesley Tyrone Proctor was born to Catherine Proctor and the late James Proctor on July 28, 1971. He is a graduate of George Washington Carver High School of Engineering and Science and is a proud member of the White-Williams Scholars Class of 1989. After high school, he received a scholarship to attend the University of Delaware. At Delaware, he received numerous awards and served on several university and community-related committees including the University of Delaware Board of Trustees.

Adding to his outstanding commitment and service at Delaware, he received his Bachelor's Degree in English with a concentration in Business and Technical Writing in 1993. After Delaware, he attended Temple University and received his Master's Degree in Education with a concentration in Higher Education Administration in 1994. Shortly after obtaining his Master's in Education, he was awarded the Dr. Marcus Foster Fellowship for outstanding academic and community service. This fellowship has funded his doctoral education at the University of Pennsylvania. At age 26, he obtained the degree of Doctor of Education from the University of Pennsylvania on May 18, 1998. His dissertation was entitled: A Piece of the Ivy: A Case Study of Black Student Retention at the University of Pennsylvania and his final defense merited distinction by his committee.

While at Penn, Wesley worked for Dr. Judith Rodin, who was the President of the University of Pennsylvania as her Speech Writer. He also served as the Director of the Master's of Arts in Teaching Program for Cheyney University. In 2003, he was appointed as the Director of Multicultural Recruitment Program for the University of Pennsylvania. Today, Dr. Proctor serves as the Executive Administrator and Youth Pastor of Victory Christian Center. He attributes all of his achievements to his Lord and Savior Jesus Christ, his spiritual father, Dr. Jimmie A. Ellis, and to his mother, Catherine Proctor. God has blessed him with a wonderful, loving and supportive mother who has always been his biggest fan. Dr. Proctor dedicates his achievements to his deceased brother, James Proctor III, who was killed in a shooting in 1988.

He is the Founder and CEO of Wesley Proctor Ministries, Inc., (founded September 2007), which is a nonprofit, 501c(3) organization dedicated to promoting spiritual and academic excellence. In addition, his organization recently awarded 19 inner city students the James William Proctor Book Award, which is a stipend that has been established to pay for graduating high school students' college semester books. Even with a demanding schedule, Wesley still finds time to mentor youth within the church and in the community.

To order additional copies of

Footprints
OF THE
FUTURE

have your credit card ready and call
1 800-917-BOOK (2665)

or e-mail
orders@selahbooks.com

or order online at
www.selahbooks.com

www.ingramcontent.com/pod-product-compliance
Lightning Source LLC
LaVergne TN
LVHW012334100826
845148LV00017B/2628

* 9 7 8 1 5 8 9 3 0 2 3 6 5 *